YOUR KNOWLEDGE HAS VALUE

- We will publish your bachelor's and master's thesis, essays and papers

- Your own eBook and book - sold worldwide in all relevant shops

- Earn money with each sale

Upload your text at www.GRIN.com
and publish for free

Bibliographic information published by the German National Library:

The German National Library lists this publication in the National Bibliography; detailed bibliographic data are available on the Internet at http://dnb.dnb.de .

This book is copyright material and must not be copied, reproduced, transferred, distributed, leased, licensed or publicly performed or used in any way except as specifically permitted in writing by the publishers, as allowed under the terms and conditions under which it was purchased or as strictly permitted by applicable copyright law. Any unauthorized distribution or use of this text may be a direct infringement of the author s and publisher s rights and those responsible may be liable in law accordingly.

Imprint:

Copyright © 2018 GRIN Verlag
Print and binding: Books on Demand GmbH, Norderstedt Germany
ISBN: 9783668626096

This book at GRIN:

https://www.grin.com/document/388685

Stanley Kavwam

Young People and the Challenge of Insecurity

Youth and Insecurity in Nigeria's Middle Belt

GRIN Verlag

GRIN - Your knowledge has value

Since its foundation in 1998, GRIN has specialized in publishing academic texts by students, college teachers and other academics as e-book and printed book. The website www.grin.com is an ideal platform for presenting term papers, final papers, scientific essays, dissertations and specialist books.

Visit us on the internet:

http://www.grin.com/

http://www.facebook.com/grincom

http://www.twitter.com/grin_com

YOUNG PEOPLE AND THE CHALLENGE OF INSECURITY: CHANGING THE NARRATIVES FOR SUSTAINABLE DEVELOPMENT IN PLATEAU STATE

Being a paper presented by Kavwam Stanley Augustine DL, BSSW, MSSW

ORGANIZED BY CENTRE FOR YOUTH PARTICIPATION, DIALOGUE AND ADVOCACY

(CYPA AFRICA)

THEME:

YOUTH, SECURITY AND GOOD GOVERNANCE: CHARTING THE WAY FORWARD FOR PLATEAU STATE

Wednesday 14th September 2016; Crest Hotel, Rayfield Road Jos Plateau State

INTRODUCTION:

I am highly delighted and indeed catapulted on top of the world to address these cultured enthusiasts of knowledge and conspicuity. The topic given to me; Young People and the Challenge of Insecurity: Changing the Narratives for Sustainable Development In Plateau State, is quite apt and pertinent in this contemporary era of unrestrained aggression across the globe amplified by the robust emergence of youths on the political landscape of Plateau State and their effective participation in the political process that culminated in the emergence of the APC government at both the State and Federal level. As a young person, I indubitably credence without any shred of pessimism that I will be able to connect with you as I share my thoughts on the above subject matter given that our destiny is inextricably tied to each other as young people who are supposedly the leaders of tomorrow. As much as I desire to divorce my brief presentation from academic underpinnings, I nevertheless sincerely confess that I am not immune from its proclivities, hence, you may find me swivel in and out of that ocean to quench our thirst as we brainstorm to change the narratives for sustainable development of Plateau State.

Youths represent the heartbeat of every society throughout history. The youthful stage of an individual's life marks the most critical and yet delicate period where the constellation of internalized habits both negative and positive are defined. These habits which are largely shaped by experiences within the individual's environment determine his/her perception and interpretation of social life. This phase of life is characterized by myriad of distractions. Distortions of reality, pressures, imbalances, angst, instabilities and insecurities just to mention a fraction; these vicissitudes predispose the youth to many vices that often than not alter the course of life either for good or bad permanently. No wonder the strength of every nation rests on the young who can either build it or destroy it.

YOUTH AND INSECURITY ON THE PLATEAU

The myriad of contestations and bloodbath witnessed over the years on the Plateau are more than religious confrontations between Muslims and Christians or even an ethnic one between the Hausa-Fulani and Berom, Jarawa (Afizere) and Anaguta. It is neither about the fear of a religious/ethnic group seeming to dominate the other. The contradictions which are daily rehearsed across the country in form of ethno-religious conflicts and fratricidal wars are rather the result of wide opportunity gabs between classes, groups and ethnic nationalities in Nigeria. It follows initially from the imposition of an exploitative colonial system, but more perniciously from the ascension of a bankrupt and degenerate indigenous leadership. This leadership has over time has failed to take strong and decisive actions that would reform and transform the colonial political economy into a self-generating and self-sustaining system that would attack inequality, unemployment and poverty. Where individuals have unequal access to resources, services and positions in society; violence, insecurity and uncertainty will be created in this process.

Insecurity is a problem common among developed and developing nations that constitute significant threat to peaceful co-existence, interaction, stability and development. It charges people with threats, tensions, anxieties and uncertainties. Examples of violent local conflicts include Tiv-Jukun, Aguleri-Amuleri, Hausa-Berom conflicts, etc. Those of international proportion include the conflict in Syria, Isreali-Palestinian, Lebanon, Iraq, Afganistan, Congo and Rwanda.

Over the years, Africa seems to have had the largest share of conflict in the world. At one point or the other, we had conflict in Algeria, Egypt, Ethiopia, Rwanda, Burundi, Nigeria, Liberia and Somalia among others. The conflicts in these countries have been devastating in terms of material and human resources; Ayitte (1999) describes the African situation as:

"Mired in steaming squalor, misery, deprivation and chaos; it is in the throes of a seemingly incurable crisis. Eating has become a luxury for many Africans, and hunger stares them squarely in the face".

At the receiving end of insecurity are sadly youths who are recruited to either fight for a cause not their own or have their educational pursuits abandoned in the wake of these violent conflicts. As a resultant consequence, the supremacy of the constitution which is the ground norm for conduct is interminably jettisoned. Farmers and herdsmen clashes have given a new definition to the dynamics of insecurity on the Plateau. This is manifested in the horrific manner in which villages are razed to rubbles over such disputes. When the constitution fails to hold accountable, perpetrators of heinous crimes owing to favoritism or selective justice, the sanctity of lives are lost. This is the fundamental precursor to youth's engagement in violent conflicts over the years with the menace of Boko Haram at the zenith of radicalization. As the nature of terrorism assumes an even dangerous dimension owing to significant advancement in technology, the future of our youths leaves a lot to be desired. This is in view of the fact that when youths are not groomed for leadership but rather occupied in destroying the future, the survival of the society beyond this generation becomes bleak and frightening. Arms stockpile and manufactured of IEDs is no longer news as many communities have been devastated by suicide bombings and hundreds of lives lost. One may be tempted to ask whether the government is unaware of these occurrences. When government seemingly tolerates the activities of lawless elements in the society, it inspires other young people to look forward to unleashing mayhem on unsuspecting members of the public with great zeal.

The basis of our harmonious coexistence as a people from time immemorial, irrespective of tribe, creed or religion has been mutual respect for one another. It is however sad to not that we are fast descending into Hobsonan state where live is brutish and short. Our youths whose creative abilities should be channeled towards the development of the nation are rather deeply inundated in creating insecurity in the country under different platforms i.e. Niger Delta Avengers, Boko Haram, MEND, Niger Delta Force, MASSOB, Fulani herdsmen etc. this precarious trend is alarming as the future looks very uncertain to the Nigerian youth in general and Plateau youth in particular. When youths engage in unrestrained destruction of critical infrastructure thus undermining the economy of the country, one wonders if at all there is any future left for those who still have an unflinching faith in the continued survival of the Nigerian nation.

Patriotism is at the lowest ebb among youth owing to decades of misrule where leaders have continually shown significant disregard for the integrity and dignity of the nation as evident in the pilfering of the nation's treasury with reckless impunity. For equity and fairness to prevail government must be seen to be unbiased in the distribution or allocation of resources e.g. herdsmen ship must or livestock rearing must be accorded equal status and recognition in terms of funding support as compared to farming of both food and cash crops as survival can be threatened without both. This stems from the fact that citizens are bound to react in certain ways and manners towards policies and programmes of government when they perceive injustice and unfairness which could be a mere figment of imagination. In this regard, government must not only be fair and just, but must be seen to be fair and just to all to forestall misinterpretations and misinterpretation by the public. The change government on the Plateau has done creditably well in curtailing some of these excesses of citizens which often undermine efforts of government in providing good governance to the public.

YOUTHS IN SCRAMBLE OVER SCARCE RESOURCES

Any disclosure on insecurity globally must commence on the premise that there is perceived injustice or inequality to be it real or imagined in the distribution of scarce social goods to which the offended party or personalities acting on their behalf undertakes to seek redress through whatever means possible often violent in nature. This is true of most agitations and contestations that have ravaged different parts of the globe. It must however, be stated that religious involvement in governance has overtime been used as a cannon fodder under which different groups hide to perpetuate violence. This position is amply demonstrated by David Sukhdeo in the following submission:

"when our social and political and national variables are mixed with religion, violence assumes an even greater role because the struggle is not fast to convert or conform to divine instructions, but also for mundane needs and wants such as social justice, racial equality, human rights, employment, financial upliftment, geographic, territories--- the list is endless--- these mundane needs and wants are issues for government to address. But religious involvement, to secular democracy – non involvement, and the degree of violence is therefore directly correlated with the level of religious involvement in the struggles for these social, political and national wants and needs." (F.E. Jimoh in Cathan 2008:81).

As opined above, several of the problems we go through in our national lives are self-inflicted in the sense that there is clear cut delineation between governance and religion as enshrined in the constitution of the Federal republic. However, political leaders go into public office with primordial and preconceived sentiments that negates the same constitution they swore to protect. Consequently, ethnicity and religious identity have emerged as major centrifugal forces threatening the survival of the Nigerian state as they are now formidable mobilization platforms than even the national anthem or pledge. Strikingly, what affects the other hence; the vicious cycle of ethno-religious contest continues to revolve with no end in sight. Unfortunately, youths are almost always in the fore front of such mobilizations and contestations. Since all the legacies bequeathed to the youth are negative, they end up replicating these negative legacies as laid down by the older generation. When we realized that our corporate existence as a people is dependent on government whom we have surrendered our security and wellbeing to manage, our conduct should reflect that understanding in patriotism. However, our tribal and religious affiliations cannot allow us extol Nigeria as our daily conduct and handling of collective resources when given the opportunity shows how despicable we treat the Nigerian nation. Tax remittances are only compelled with as a matter of choice not obligation. As a result, the needed resources to endanger development by government are not available. If we must progress as a nation, we must pull down the barriers we have erected that barricaded us from one another so we can relate as Nigerians first before whatever considerations there may be. If the constitution of the federal republic is the rallying point for all Nigerians, then it must be borne in mind that customary land ownership which has often given rise to violent conflicts as witnessed on the Plateau, is guaranteed under the same constitution and as such should be respected except where an amendment to that provision is made. This is in view of the fact that political leaders, who are saddled with the responsibility of upholding the constitution, often engrossed in sectional sentiments, tend to jettison this clear and unambiguous provision thereby leaving the illiterate segment of the public in unimaginable bloodbath over land.

BREAKING THE CONUNDRUM OF RELIGIOUS IDENTITY

The problem of Nigerian society is the error of attributing to religious motive what may be an expression of a purely secular and political viewpoint. According to Agi (1999) *"some of what conventional wisdom tags as religious in Nigeria has nothing to do with religion, or at best has only tangential relation with it"*

Closely related to the above is religious fanaticism or extremism, which is essentially a negative and vicious attitude towards religion, characterized by exaggerations, immoderation, manipulation, exploitation, excesses and violence. Iwe (2000,PP:132) further points out that;

> *"Religion is essentially and fundamental a spiritual issue and exercise.*
>
> *It arises from man's consciousness and practical acknowledgement of*
>
> *His dependence on God (the absolute and ultimate reality) and from his*
>
> *Search for answers to the basic universal non-material issues of human*
>
> *Existence"*

Nigeria is a country bedeviled with not only religious violence but also political instability, sophisticate crimes, ethic militia groups, hired killings, kidnapping, discrimination against women, incidents of mission people and ethnic conflicts. As a country that is more than 55 years now, many concerned citizens have often reflect on Nigeria's slow rate of development, poverty and socio-economic crisis. A lot of people point accusing fingers on leadership. The famous writer (Chinua Achebe 1985) has to this to say,

> *"The trouble with Nigeria is simply and squarely a failure of leadership.*
>
> *There is nothing wrong with the Nigerian character. There is nothing*
>
> *Wrong with Nigerian climate or land or water or air or anything else.*
>
> *The Nigeria problem is the unwillingness or inability of its leaders to rise*

To the responsibility, to the challenge of personal example which is the

Hall mark of true leadership"

Nigeria is a country with pluralism of various kinds – cultural, ethnic, linguistic, religious, political, economy and philosophical pluralisms. Dialogue becomes necessary and relevant in this complex society. Pluralism should be utilized for sustainable growth and development.

Dialogue is extremely important that no person, group, culture, institution or religion can escape it. According to Okuke (2000:88) dialogue, which brings peace, unity harmony, development and progress, is a good means to break the barrier between peoples of different culture, language, history and geographical location.

As Martin Luther King Jnr. Resonates even in death:

Returning hate for hate multiples hate, adding deeper darkness to a night

Already devoid of stars. Darkness cannot drive out hate, only love can do

That. Hate multiples hate: violence multiples violence and toughness

Multiples toughness in a descending spiral destruction.

Insecurity as other social problems is part of the legacy everyone receives along with their membership of society. Thus, perplexing new situations constantly arise. Frequently, tensions and strains arise in the family, neighborhoods, community and the society at large. It is not uncommon for a group that seeks to avoid problems by holding to tried and tested rules to find its life hopelessly complicated by changes that are external to it. Social problems arise from social needs. Some of these needs like clothing, food and shelter, are more basic while others, like needs are not met, they give rise to uncertainty which the society has to grapple with. The problems of poverty frequently leads to several other social problems such as restiveness, armed robbery, juvenile delinquency, drug addiction and drug trafficking, malnutrition, disease, prostitution etc. though there is no single direct relationship between poverty and crime, it can nevertheless make crime more severe in a neighborhood or community.

YOUTH ORGANISED VIOLENT BEHAVIOUR IN NIGERIA

Since Nigeria's return to civil rule in 1999, disturbances, contestations and violence are unrelenting, about which the print media in Nigeria have besieged the readership with screaming headlines on exploding bouts of civil disturbances (Alubo,2008). An analyst summed the situation by stating that *"we are passing through an era when Nigerians could hardly make up their minds as to just what sort of country they really aspired to erect"* (Uwazurike 2003:79).

Following from the above, Nigerians are becoming injured to streets and countryside enveloped in putrid smell of decomposing corpses, thousands fleeing for safety, as well as the sights of charred and desolate buildings as civil disturbances have become both recurrent and frequent. Armed no-state groups have significantly undermined the country's internal security environment largely using young men as foot soldiers. Among these groups, Boko Haram has grown to become a serious national, regional and international concern. Estimate of the death tool, from Boko Haram attacks since 2009, range as high as ten thousand fatalities. With Boko Haram and other groups seemingly gaining strength, questions arise as to why young men join them in the first place. Surveys, interviews and focus groups discussions conducted in 2003 by the United State Institute of Peace, suggest that poverty, unemployment, illiteracy and weak family structure makes or contribute to making young men vulnerable to radicalization. Itinerant preachers capitalize on the situation by preaching an extreme version of religion and conveying a narrative of the government as weak and corrupt. Armed groups such as the Boko Haram can recruit and train youths for activities ranging from errand running to suicide bombings (Alubo, 2008).

ETHNICITY AS DIVISIVE PHENOMENON

Ethnicity is conundrum that relatively influences the perspective and practice of Nigerians in all spheres of human existence; "we Yoruba's and those Hausa's, we Igbo's and those Fulani's, we Berom"s and those Mwaghavul's, we Tarok and those Jukun"s. such conceptualizations take place in many social, political and economic situations, and they help to maintain and structure the boundaries of culture and interaction. Despite changes that have taken places since European colonization, Mercier (1986:14) maintained that: *"the boundaries between ethnic groups have been able to retain or assume great significance"*. It affects where one lives, with whom one associates, for whom one votes, at what occupation one works and so forth. Although the enclaves may be geographical realities, it is of great concern that they are behavioral realities.

The nature of European scramble for Africa and it subsequent portion among European countries have had important consequences for the independent states of the continent. The artificial boundaries of the state, which emerged from European imperial expansion, have salient implications for political development in these states. After independence, one saw the Hausa of Nigeria with members of their family living together as citizens of Niger republic. The Ewes are split between Ghana and Togo; Yoruba's are found across the borders of Nigeria and Benin republic; Somalis found themselves in Kenya, Somalia and Ethiopia; and the same goes for the Massai in Tanzania and Kenya. It is therefore not surprising that peaceful coexistence and harmony in most African counties have been punctuated by irredentist movements. These artificial boundaries created culturally diverse states as they brought together strange ethno-cultural groups into one political territory . the problem of integration arising from these have been amply demonstrated by communal/religious instability and/or secessionist bids in Sudan ,Rwanda, Zaire, Burundi, Zanzibar, Uganda, Nigeria, the chad and Angola.

CONCLUSION

The task at present is to respond to the crisis of nation-state project, and in confronting the task, necessary starting point must be the recognition of the country's pluralism and the cultivation of diversity as the building blocks of unity (Egwu S. 2001). In this reconstruction, the state democracy must engage the ethnic and religious conundrum by exploring virtues of dialogue, negotiation and consensus building. Similarly, the constitution must address the question of citizenship and indigneity with the commitment to build a national citizenship. While privileges attached to 'state of origins' cannot be wished away, efforts must be made to build and promote national integration as precondition for accessing all rights and privileges of 'indigenes' for Nigerians who reside in places other than ethnic homelands and fulfill their obligations of citizenship that discourage any discrimination across the country.

If this democratic context is to offer any meaningful answer to the fears and anxieties that trigger negative ethnic and religious mobilization, particularly the use of young people as foot soldiers to unleash terror, it should assign a leading role to the state whose excesses are to be curbed and challenged by virile civil society. And it has to be *'social democracy'* anchored on redistribution of wealth.

On a finale note, I crave the indulgence of my fellow Plateau youths to resist whatever trappings or inducement from self-seeking persons or groups to enslave us under the guise of loyalty while in fact we are being used as thugs to cause mayhem in the society. The society needs you to contribute your own quota to making it a better place. Why destroy our tomorrow by actions or inactions we undertake today when the survival of Plateau depends on us? May we strive to build character and reputation that is hinged on excellence, uncommon patriotism, meritocracy and unyielding faith in the plateau dream as envisioned by our immortal sage. As the future awaits us with medals, I see us emerging as a spring in the wilderness, an oasis in the dessert, an eagle souring against the tempest storm to reclaim our lost glory and Plateau shall rise again traversing tracts never charted by civilization or people in the past or present.

REFERENCES

Alubo S.O (2008) Ethnic Conflicts and Citizenship Crises in the Central Region, Ibadan. Programme on Ethnic and Federal Studies.

Egwu S. (1999), The Agrarian Question, Politics and Ethnicity in Rural Nigeria. Centre for Advanced Social Sciences (CASS).

Agi S.P.I (1999), Holy Violence, Religion and Global Disorder, Makurdi, Editors Ehi.

Achebe C. (1985), The Problem with Nigeria, Enugu: Fourth Dimension Publishing.

Ayittey G.B.N (1999), African on Chaos, New York, St. Martins Press.

CATHAN, (2008), Religion, Violence and Conflict Resolution in Nigeria, Makurdi Aboki Publishers.

Dahl R. (1999) Who Governs: Yale University Press

Egwu S. (1999), The Agrarian Question, Politics and Ethnicity in Rural Nigeria. Centre for Advanced Social Sciences (CASS).

Odey J.O. (1995) Martin Luther King; His Life Message (Second Edition) Enugu, SNAAP Press.

Iwe N.S.S. (2000), Religious Fanaticism, Causes, Consequences and Remedies, Calabar, Sales Print Publisher.

The Boko Haram Uprising and Islamic Revivalism in Nigeria. Africa Spectrum, 45 (2), 95-110

Okuke B.O. (2000). The Practice of Sharia in Nigeria; A Democratic Secular State. ENUGU ASAAP Press

Omoregbe J.I (2000) "Christianity and Islam in Dialogue: In Agwanorobo Eruubetine (ed), The Humanism Management of Pluralism; A Formular for Development in Nigeria, Lagos, Mutab Press."

Ottite O. (1989), Ethnic Plurality and Ethnicity in Nigeria (Ibadan). Vintage Press.

YOUR KNOWLEDGE HAS VALUE

- We will publish your bachelor's and master's thesis, essays and papers

- Your own eBook and book - sold worldwide in all relevant shops

- Earn money with each sale

Upload your text at www.GRIN.com
and publish for free